CONCENTRIC CIRCLES

YANG LIAN

CONCENTRIC CIRCLES

TRANSLATED BY
BRIAN HOLTON
& AGNES HUNG-CHONG CHAN

BLOODAXE BOOKS

Copyright © Yang Lian 1999, 2005
Translation copyright © Brian Holton & Agnes Hung-Chong Chan 2005

ISBN: 978 1 85224 703 4

First published 2005 by
Bloodaxe Books Ltd,
Eastburn,
South Park,
Hexham,
Northumberland NE46 1BS.

www.bloodaxebooks.com
For further information about Bloodaxe titles
please visit our website and join our mailing list
or write to the above address for a catalogue.

Supported using public funding by
ARTS COUNCIL
ENGLAND

Digital reprint by Lightning Source.

ACKNOWLEDGEMENTS

Concentric Circles was first published in Chinese by Shanghai Wenyi Press in 1999. The translation of Chapter One appeared in *Poetry London*, 44 (Spring 2003).

Brian Holton and Agnes Hung-Chong Chan would like to thank the Translation Centre in the Department of Chinese and Bilingual Studies at Polytechnic University of Hong Kong for a series of grants to assist the work of translating *Concentric Circles*. They also thank their friend and colleague and friend Dr Chu Chiyu for his constant support and advice.

Special thanks are due to Arts Council England for providing a translation grant for this book.

CONTENTS

TALKING

EARTH

INCH

Moved Once Again by an Ancient Betrayal
– by way of a Preface to *Concentric Circles*

When the Chinese translation of Ezra Pound's *Pisan Cantos* was published, I wrote a short essay for it, entitled *In the Timeless Air*, in which I came to a sensational conclusion: only with its Chinese translation was the *Cantos* finally completed. The argument is not actually complicated. To me, the most impressive poetic quality of the *Cantos* lies in the contradiction between the synchronic nature of its poetic ideas and the diachronic nature of its language. The startlingly, inexplicably large-scale collage of episodes that seems out of control cannot be obviously explained by Pound's simple intention to write the longest poem in English. I think Pound's real focus was to break through the limitations of time, especially those temporal limits which exist in the grammar of English. His *Cantos* ramify through all time – it is by embracing all cultures, past to present, East and West, that he is enabled to cut out the differentiation between the presentation of life in various ways, and touch directly on the changeless core.

In other words, the *Cantos* is not an epic: rather, it uses poetry to efface the diachronic mirage. That self-sufficient universe of poetry, without beginning or end, completely overthrows the European epic tradition. I do not know whether this creative idea of Pound's derived from his "reinvention" of ancient Chinese poetry. But the Chinese language does give him the best reward of all: by way of the constant form of Chinese verbs – which are unchanged, even if person and tense change – the Chinese translation of the *Cantos* eradicates all trace of the struggle between the poet and the language, and completes Pound's success in breaking away from the diachronic grip of the English language. What the Chinese reader sees is the *Cantos* re-invented via the unique qualities of the Chinese language, an entirety which is transparent, stable, omnipresent and flawless. In the timeless air, the poems themselves are the air.

I should be happy that, when I started to write the long poem *Concentric Circles* in 1994, my "Yanglish" was far too bad to read the *Cantos* in its original language, and that the *Pisan Cantos* were not published in China until 1998: I could therefore avoid the suspicion of having produced a Chinese version of the *Cantos* in my *Concentric Circles*. The poetic space of *Concentric Circles* is achieved precisely by deleting time in order to highlight the human condition, which remains essentially the same despite all apparent change. This idea comes from my awareness of the still treacherous blood ties between the reality of China and the nature of the Chinese language.

To me, synchronisation is not a metaphysical game, but a kind of necessity rooted in the connotative meaning of my writings. However, the problem now, as I write this preface to the English translation of *Concentric Circles*, is whether Brian Holton and Agnes Chan's English – after it has been compelled to make clear the person of verbs and choose their tense, as well as define nouns as singular or plural – will open the sealed magic box, or break an exquisite piece of porcelain? I remember how Brian used to embarrass me with this kind of question, which was something I had never been asked before. But I have to say I like this kind of embarrassment. It compels me to see those things which originally were hidden on an indistinct level within the Chinese text. It is like the Chinese translation of the *Cantos* in reverse, in which Brian and Agnes are pulling back my work into the diachronic conflict, examining each line from the perspective of time and tense, finding and exposing the internal relationships between the lines, and so testing the credibility of the synchronic factors there. Such an act is linguistic in nature, and at the same time directly concerned with existence itself. With the linguistic layers which translation creatively adds, the challenge that the original text poses becomes more risky, more varied, and more beautiful. Therefore, the English translation is not the finish, but a new beginning for *Concentric Circles*, which will continue its adventures in all the other non-Chinese diachronic languages. I converse with Pound in *Concentric Circles*, 'moved once again by an ancient betrayal', and I think he would have liked this idea.

When my exile began in 1989, the challenge that I was faced with was not only 'why should I write', but 'how should I write?' In other words, was it possible for me, instead of refusing to progress beyond the stage of discussing my own exile, to continue developing creativity in poetic form, to match my so-called "profound" experiences? For a Chinese poet, this also in and of itself included the bigger proposition: how could poetry written during my exile add to the modern transformation of the entire tradition of Chinese verse? The poetry ought to be deeper, not just different.

Where the Sea Stands Still, written in 1993, is composed of several poem cycles, a structure that I used for the first time outside China. Later, I called this kind of writing the discovery of a 'structure of life'. *Concentric Circles*, written between 1994 and 1997, brought the formal elements of *Where the Sea Stands Still* into full play. I am even tempted to say the form of *Concentric Circles* is more "man-made" – as flawless as the musical structure of a seven-syllable regulated verse.[1]

First, the whole book is similar to a complete geometric form: there are five chapters altogether (linked to each other by the progressively increasing number of circles), and in each chapter, there are three sections. Second, the inner structure is asymmetric and steady: the relatively "abstract" thinking in the first, third and fifth chapters, and the concrete autobiographical content in the second and fourth chapters pile on top of each other, constituting a multi-storey space both varied and unified. Here, the choice of 'Concentric Circles' as the title and the structure seems to be destined by some imperceptible but inexorable reason.

On the one hand, it developed out of ideas begun long ago when I wrote the long poem *Yi*.[2] On the other hand, it grew out of seemingly pure chance: an artist friend of mine took a photo when she worked on her piece *Do Angels Really Exist?* – in an almost completely dark room, the light emitted from the only small bulb broadened into a set of concentric circles on the ground. It was strange not only because the photo captured something invisible to the naked eye (a kind of ghost?), but because it seemed to unveil a hidden structure deep down in the world, which provided the omnipresent darkness with a structure, or a mode. The darkness could not be manifest without it. I introduced this image directly into a prose poem in chapter three. But the darkness formed into 'concentric circles' went far beyond the room. It extended limitlessly, embracing all my experiences of life: self/other, in China/out of China, contemporaneity/historicity, real life/writing, existence/illusion, internality/externality, and so on...and then it penetrated me, pointing toward the essential human condition. Three years of writing entered *Concentric Circles* into the ranks of *Yi* and *Where the Sea Stands Still*, forming the keel of my own "mini-tradition", and that is precisely what we would expect it to be: the roots of the living tradition of Chinese poetry.

Much contemporary Chinese poetry gives Western readers the impression of surrealism. But to me, such playing with imagery so obscure it's straightforward is actually a diminishment of real writing. All of my efforts to write *Concentric Circles* were focused on "deep reality". The choice of form in each line and each poem and the impetus to create the whole book, all originated from my own interrogation of the human condition. I owe a debt of gratitude to my Chinese experiences. (Which I plainly call 'nightmare inspiration'.) Cruel reality, the eccentric circles of history, heavy cultural burdens, the obstacles to linking our culture with "mainstream" Western culture, and our ancient language, which serves as the double source of both destruction and rebirth, all reveal for me how many levels there are in that so-called "depth". When people talk about 'the pains of time' in China with feigned profundity, they do not know the reality is much more horrible than that: what I want to express in my works is exactly 'the pain of timelessness'.

The "history" of China is just like a square black Chinese character, which, time or tense notwithstanding, never changes. This brings us back to Pound again. As a matter of fact, not only did he "invent" ancient Chinese poetry for the West, but, for Chinese poets, he also re-invented the Chinese language. I mean that he invented an attitude towards one's own language, so that the Chinese characters could shed their barbaric primitivity (a kind of vulgar "mystery"?) and become the organic material poets could use to signify a certain poetic image that could not be expressed by anything else. You may say that the fifth circle of *Concentric Circles* is Chinese-language conceptual art: I divided the Chinese character 詩 ('poetry') into its three constituent parts (言 土 寸 – each of which is a character by itself), and used each of them to develop a set of seven poems with a single-character title containing the same radical; the three sets are all ended with a poem entitled 詩 .

These twenty-one poems together compose a "world inside a character". They are connected to each other by the visual element of their titles (the first level of Chineseness, or the nature of the Chinese language), and then in the poems, I further deal with various levels of Chineseness and Chinese poetry: visual, auditory, the absence of marked person, the absence of marked tense, homonyms, the use of characters to mark sounds, palindromes, the use of allegory, radicals serving as independent characters, two-dimensional reading, unfinished lines...so questioning the language to an extreme, and unfolding it again at the end of my questioning. Please do not forget the last unfinished line of the book: poem is – what?

This open question is directly inherited from *Heavenly Questions* written by Qu Yuan[4] two thousand, five hundred years ago. Do time and "evolution" really bring anything to our life – when we still suffer from the pain of not finding any answers?

The English translation of *Concentric Circles* is a pagoda built from the top. What Brian and Agnes did here was not to give Western readers another brochure for the cultural tourist, but to challenge both themselves and the reader. They could hardly find any similar work translated from Chinese to which they could have referred. (I have to say that, translation to or from Chinese falls very short when compared with translation to or from European languages.) This blankness compelled them to invent! For the reader, this translation perfectly manifests the quality of poetry itself: the refusal to give in to vulgarity. I am happy that *Concentric Circles* still retains its flavour of "ancient betrayal" even in translation. My effort to exceed the limits of the Chinese language was "translated" by Brian and Agnes into creativity in English. This is how it ought to be, because I am moved once again when I read the translation, and I feel that I am struggling free from time and am incorporated into the beautiful 'concentric circles' of ancient and modern poetry, in China or elsewhere.

YANG LIAN
London

1. The *lüshi*, a classical Chinese form with a strict tonal pattern and rhyme scheme, and seven syllables per line. [Tr.]

2. (Xiandai Shi She, Taipei, 1994); tr. Mabel Lee, *Yi* (Green Integer, København/ Los Angeles, 2002). [Tr.]

3. Meaning, respectively, 'speech/talking' 'earth' 'sky' [Tr.]

4. The famous minister in the Kingdom of Chu during the period of the Warring States (475–221 BC), who was later banished to the distant south and finally threw himself into Miluo River to show his loyalty. [Tr.]

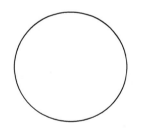

Chapter One

1.

fear of cold left behind by the cold
pale height of rocks left behind by blindness of rocks
ear-piercing autumn   by atrophied trees
subtracted from between the tree-trunks

then wind   not among withered branches but human bones only
not fruit skin but decayed hearing only
not to scour wings but to scour bright the age-old chorus of metals only

the dead fire through dense fog   leaving death behind
empty fields   dark vision where furrows emit the smell of stew
frozen stiff walnuts twisted off one by one
among addresses of wine by the glass   an ocean colourful and cruel
every minute empties out a cathedral where our fears are stored

subtracted   down to the sum of destruction

2.

there is always what's heard vaguely in a dim corridor
buzzing in the ears   moves far away outside the ears

at the sea-level of stone
sound   breaking up the chord of bird bone
chases in reverse a body that can feel pain
our bodies born again and again by a pair of pink organs

reality always intensified   gushes out from a tunnel of wind
a thousand cacti married to a composer's night
from high above goats' empty orbits exceed our air

sound moves away   ears smashed to pieces

3.

fear   between valley and valley the hydatiform mole brewing
fear   between gold and golden
                      ruins of man
pipe organ shine   wades across the river pissed by a bedwetting baby
sunshine   lifelong silence dropped by a cloud
                    what's heard
always kneads the flame of pubic hair between sleeps
between days   a stomach sweats in the midnight sky
silence   opens the dark score of granite

fear our fearlessness   between mountain roads
sharp reeds of bird have no fear of scratching the morning
sit   fear no chair
got to rely on white bones sticking out of fingertips
                    pay attention to the show
old women's weeping guts dazzlingly bright
face carved into inscription   the more you listen the more like your own
blood resonating in a wax rainstorm
                    old women's weary knees
stick close   thrashing   countless dull red inflamed knees
choir   kneels on a glass rose with no fear
allow brown tongues to lick out the dew
fear no shame   so do your best to reproduce

we who are reproduced by fear   build a mountain peak
                    be heard by what can never hear and
become   the tenderest between ghost and ghost
between talking and talking white snow brilliant in four seasons
exposes the body's absolute zero of linguistics
                    confirmed by deathly pale flaws
between blue wrinkled wombs   a distance that cannot be filled

4.

poetry   impossibly not universal surrender
tongues beat the drum's surface   impossibly
without hitting truth

those unwilling to be freeze-framed   are fixed in a snowstorm lit by candlelight
read by nostril-terrifying smell of salt fish
the porno sky that lusts for death row convicts is reading
the map   bored now with reading

those stranded in the golden brain
every day   push a dead concrete wall to the deaf

the knife that excised us rehearses heart-beats on the plate

impossibly   the living aren't part of fallen leaves under the trees
butterfly pinned on the wall impossibly not a peacock
dawdle   death is the only garden
impossible not to excrete weddings on Saturday's meadows
thundering kisses   endlessly glued to make stones that bomb the eyes

when speech is left behind by speechless   life's last day is
left behind by days   a greasy window on no direction
unpassable   exhibits the only collapse

5.

autumn vibrates between nows like a crazy musical instrument

in golden Mass memory shrinks
bodies   when reviewed by a beam of light between bodies
we   are mud flow taking fiery red breath

only when faces are fate is then the now

lungs   pull tight a black maximum deeper than us
beasts carefully cover the silver-white calcium in bones
a distance in illness
when unreachable   is seen by this rancid belch
blinded   then pressed under an ocean paperweight   written out

hounds fiercely barking   driving the now into a word
wordless   only thus the now is left over

a mountain stores the weight of the music it endures through its life
a pipe organ puts in false teeth to lie
saying   flesh with no breach   cold white arpeggio overnight gone far away
voiceless   sow the glittering wheat grains of dead bugs

subtraction   grammar that organises a lonely army
using our eyes   to organise sunlight's depleted pain
beat up a berry till the pus it deposited quietly turns purple
testicles hanging in solitude   deleting the now from reality

Chapter Two

UNTIL

until sky is like a breast popping out from a collar
held by horrible hands   your hands
until slow death   displays more distinct violence

until a dead drunk fiddle has just shed its feathers
until a bird flies into the snow-white structure of its own skull
a pair of fleshless orbits stare outside the window

staring   wind   twelve months' paralysed blood
thick smoke in the fireplace always seems like the last time
blackening a horrible throat   your throat

remembrance   not remembering until transparent
another   each flung broken-necked elsewhere
storm   until the tiny storm-storing heart

use more distinct violence   display slow death
this horrible rotting   your rotting
like a zero with no exit

like a scream   expanding its territory until tonight
tonight   expanding its face out to the belly-tattooed ocean
sea given to a golden frame until

painless   severer than headache
the entire sky a nail that can never be pulled
but is hammered home   until this bird's head undyingly rots into thinking

until nobody can reach the finish
until the impossible   always uses you to flood the finish
until slow death   wakes you at midnight

wind   twelve months' paralysed blood displays more distinct violence
until your head is the only horror
fleshless and snow-white   until   your mud splatters all over

THEN

then you go on dying   dying in plaster
then the pitch-black snow inside the womb goes on falling
then the face is not while burning pain on the face is

wound is not while the ripe age preserved by beheading is
staying awake is not but sleeping more than a century is
eyelids   oozed the blue of eyes

then even mask is not
in the candlelight   facial features are an early-winter field
a plaster apple is summoning the pitch-black apple trees

a plaster baby is summoning the dead through clenched gums
then a sleigh full of audiences for four seasons drives in
sky is not   crow's signature suddenly is

the sound of snow moving upon tiles
the smallest crystal bedroom   when tongue licks into you
skin absolutely is not   then lovers

all like a stone-paved town hanging inside you
then go on being loved   with fragile beauty in the moment of death
then getting drunk is not while a glass of wine for ever is

a million women moulded by a womb
exquisitely designed tower   shut in the open sunshine
with you   can only be

with nothing   then must be
a numb look again and again moulded by an adverb
a poem moulds a wall of disgust that chases humans

then golden patience no longer is
then   plaster roses when unpluckable forever must be anything but
the post-mortem summoned by your funeral make-up   then the funeral goes on

SINCE

since the undated   neglected foul blood's due date
since the year fell off a bed's edge   edged you out
since conceiving evil   itself conceived

what wraps two dripping fruit segments   wraps a present too
since solitude became your food
name   turns you into your own tenant

since those turning their back on age   turned back to a birthday
since the nookied cloud   sat on a naked spiral stair
dazzlingly blue sex of a tigress   surged to your sex

countless sunken ships show their masts above the town's sea surface
since anchors of survival   hooked onto the forehead
corpses have been pulling a net

since the soul that pressed you so hard   pressed so near night at four p.m.
since the dark green meadow has filled with a white horse's bitter jealousy
since having lived   like impure death lived

name   turns you into your own tenant
directions   always patted off a dirty pillow
bad dreams dreaming the limit of four limbs

a flesh-coloured ATM drawer   draws again the you of now
the gleaming fish of an ambulance   carries away your now
since every minute abandons those in the minute of childbirth

from now to now   broken bones in a thumb joint a far journey
since rape could never end
since your illness   projected an endless you

life   trains people to love the shame dearly
since   destruction set off from far away to return to your own destruction
a tooth not refusing to be buried refuses the theme of time

Chapter Three

whoever is ruin will open wide the golden cranium
whoever is destroyed   will embrace starlight's knowledge
heavy snow again   directly falls in between invisible seats
ashes   scattered in a man's skeleton
the dead's glances everywhere
excited a drop of water   madly growing into silver-white carnivorous grass
after death   madly grows through our broken walls

whoever has stony orbits can endlessly hurt the sky
whoever sits into a blaze's centenary   is listening

pipe organ   boiling oil still trickling down five unspread golden fingers
boy's sintered glass is trickling
between nothingnesses   sound of wind   ghosts' violent imaginings

pipe organ flying along corpses
has angelic eccentricity   making what never vanishes in cold

whoever listens   then has heard

stone's previous life   emptied flesh and blood out to abandon the mould
stone's stalk   penetrates winter to retain the torment
between storm clouds of stones our caresses climb a crying fit

one drop of semen sucked tight by female warmth in the sky's body
one cluster of eggs   hanging   the darkness in which maggots nest
one hundred kidneys turn into vocalists for the rustling moon

whoever has lived in snow-covered places then walks the tip of a madman's tongue

the proposition of limitlessness   limitlessly pushes into an instant
twilight a proposition   gathering the blaze's meditation between collapsed vaults
fable's flesh in every age
all roasted   a cathedral from snowstorm to snowstorm
mercilessly sieved by madly grown light
a man from here to here   listens to one night limitlessly festering

                                        whoever is left behind by time
                                        will build up a prison of time

by   an instant of love-lying the pipe organ is uprooted

music isn't here   this speeding ear robs us
on music's vast foundation
heavy fog exhaled from this mouth disperses a century's audience
until   limitlessness tightens harm into a colourless pupil
then   whoever hugs the sky too tight will be endlessly set out on this time
since   nothing left inside us

between us   the pipe organ expressionlessly smashes another life

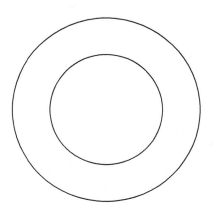

IT WAS

it was in father's pebbly womb   waiting
it was waiting in a head's huge tide   to be born
it was born under a coffin of character   kneeling to say

      don't want days

it was hearing the same endless blood-red storm of ribs
it was the flesh sounding the full moon fiddle   loudly weeping
it was weeping a river of long-sighted glasses   mourning
witnessing its own pitch-dark back   in   another now

      don't want days that represent ends

hospital's white snow   ignoring a ray of light's refusal   carries on the surgery
five-finger tower   combed through a million babies' white hair that called for help
this winter in agony   draws a profile of frozen passion
I live in the body of that man called father

      don't need what death once strongly demanded

it was   a furiously stamping calf squeezed into another man's belly
it was eliminating warm distance on the last delivery bed

JANUARY OF THE DEAD

father   cuts this blackest month from a year
January   afternoon music in mothers' blindness

bell of an old-fashioned alarm clock has rung for twenty years in the blink of an eye
frozen stiff shoes   flung for twenty years on the dawn-iced road
feet   trembling guts of little trembling beasts
the meadow's nerve-collapsing green   staying awake for twenty years
old clothes hanging   yet ashes stolen
twenty Januarys   bloodline of dark windows

father   excises this skyless month in a year

mothers echo   candlelight   so fragile that it pricks
mother   when she's most lonely   accompanies herself to death
covers January   blankets dirty snow of roadside-huddling children

overnight gales catch what even wounds can't confirm
carved into twenty panes of glass   twenty drops of half-falling tears
twenty times   sneer at our ignorance of death

7 MULINEN STRASSE

when pain hugs a baby tight   sweetness is an inborn flaw
coolness of an ivory bracelet fills with murderous intent
and a white balcony   has learned to be rain-drenched
highlight blood   a link too unreliable

more unreliable than death is
more like milk regurgitated than the one-year-old sky is
more lust retained than the womb has

flying   over-bright butterflies fly out of the fissure

before the entrance to the next life   will the dead shiver
remember this newly-shaped pink phlegm or not
desperately avoiding the sound of rain in the bathtub
unable to avoid   the pillow bleached by all-night sex

when a looking balcony is being looked at
swans lost every day in thoughts of flowing water

father   overgrown one-year-old park still waits out there
we are carried in the arms to this side of the skin
expelled by the hostile glass eye of an empty wine bottle
returning   learned from a melting mare how to breathe

MIDNIGHT LETTER

I've used up all my midnights
writing   I've used up
all the darkness locked up by a lamp
writing down   total lunar eclipse daughter sets out from white paper skin

a golden storm just formed in the brain

a letter written at nil o'clock   nil that's flowing in the blood
grip all the past with five fingers
clouds   masses of loneliness solidified into concrete
sky   the daughter unearths the phosphorus dying in each word's heart
then human bones   are hurt by an address's wounds
my midnight   semen spurted into blankness

long used up   the flesh-coloured ocean with no recipient
no bodies but only the reproductive hostility of bodies

no love   but the eyes lusting for insomnia to be destroyed
so dazzling the midnight despair in a girl
unchanging   nil used up all my ghosts

THE GARDEN OF TRANSMIGRATION

a crowd walking with faces half bitten off
a crowd of destruction walking
walk into sunlight   the lingering scent of dead marble

on an obscene map   bird pins are stuck
wind   non-reality digs a big tree root
the bleak lust of bleak sky

direction in which stars explode   baring the flowers
direction in which rabbits madly run   a hunter's empty chair
shooting today into today's patch of weeds
below ground   heavy snowfall illumines a dark maximum
what's rotted   father   lets us caress

a dream   enfolding a head brighter yet since death
no memory   no road
no   crowds lay bare the smell of blood under poison sunlight
the garden has never vanished   with one touch the garden mercilessly resurrects

LIFE   THIS WORD

this is only a way to live   sound chewed in the mouth
death too is a way to live   sound chews the mouth
similar sound from two hara-kiri fish bellies someone chewed

you cast off this forty-year-old apparel and I have put it on

this word   this spot of long-emitted sperm
casting   this skin   so hard   so coarse
nerves   blood   dream   stick on bones
                    syllable's four limbs
                    bound to the sickbed
you cast off this forty-year-old face   while
mine   seethes in a pot laughing madly for forty years
talking is writing   writing is boiling

and boiling is living

                    fish words
are only   the vile weather stomach-matured
you cast off your covering of snow-white salt   ocean stands at my end
this bone marrow hears each instant rot twice
bed bites all the bodies only once
a set of glass guts   rinse   blood-red waterfall cascading down spring
                    chewing
false teeth   flashing details of lies

※

breachless bodies can only wait
   skin   flayed in one piece
                crawl   rub on pink sand

no crying   organs echo all night
             for the whole night
             moonlight has been eliminating the souls of the dead
  flowers reproduce bits of broken eyes
  in dense silver fog   gaze can't disperse

each disastrous day being gazed
             has roots of flesh
             is like flesh   unavoidable

even gentler wind is enough to make us twitch
so similar the beauty   so huge the molluscs
madness   distance after the rain
             waiting   undying
             all night the moonlit asphalt doesn't sleep

look   days come by way of bodies   that language directly hits the wound

look   naked to the end

             who isn't a bloody dripping tail
             is savagely swung by pain

  crawl   can't crawl away from our own hideous claws
  under moonlight   everywhere the locked-in stones are tears

※

you   I   sound of rain   October droops between the legs   ocean
turn a page   morning unwilling to wake   squeezed   every year
endure   a little heat   grows bit   by bit   once imagined missing another
bus   window   tongue erects   the world's obstacles
I   bright definition   morning's most unthinking part
gentleness   days   days' absolutely painful gentleness   one
leg   press down on those legs   white   entreat   two minutes

at their last gasp they cry for mother   expanse of white snow   recycling bag
twisting tight   sweet tiger on butterfly body   omit   by chance
mother   from ward to ward   leukemic map   drawn dry
chopped up   bile blackish green   I'm cuddled   miss once
unknown white hair   mother   always in the morning   nose
layer by layer transparent   the last   at first   when too hot it's about
vagina   not confronting death will one still fear time so much   save me

experiencing a cellular reality a reality unwilling to wake up at morning tell or
can't tell or impossible to tell when you can't not tell experience you're not blank
you make your own blankness dazzlingly threatening a blood-red eyeball glares
at lifelong illogical scenery
                              live   no word

with no   with only   no   only   with no
no with   this place   which place   this   with
no no   only only   only   this
which   no   with no with   which place   not
is   this place   this place with no this place   this
place with only this place   is not   not which   not
place   which is this place   is not which place   is
only is   not only is   only not is   with no
with only   is not is   with no this place with only which
place   which   is   which is not   which no
this is   this not   this place   the stink of breathing

※

only a way to live   in breachless body
            body is the only illusion
only a way to speak   like not to speak or being spoken
            words   twist tight the blood-stagnated throat

death is an ironic statement   stamp
bright red for mailing baby ears

            you strip off your darkness
            baring me   paralysed on organs

no   only   fingers poked into the past
            are all poked right by the past
nobody there   sky's cruel garden endlessly moves to another patch of
blue   no more no less confirming the shame of eyes
you strip   the lifelong debts that can't be stripped away
            and so I'm owed
in stuttered womb   that fills with fruit's sweet and fishy
greasy   iron-grey résumé on which harm is far from enough
death   the more densely it vomits children the less they are enough

this sunlight   how many times of return will be enough to destroy it in an instant

the crowd   walking   where
            transmigrate to a man's depth
which   body   place   endures   the masturbating golden inscription

            four seasons   solitary form brighter still
            a thousand years at forty
you strip off this nailed fast coffin and I wake up in it
listen   when you stick tight to white bones   quietly listening
disgust   is only what's got by the waiting concrete flower
I'm   still an incident in a word without the power to happen
            still alive   still
            unspoken

IT IS

it is really the ocean   that forms a drop of ink all around me
it is really the rock's purplish red nipple   on four pitch-black walls

    it is   striving towards pain with this year
    someone's five fingers melt in the hollow of my palm
    snow of the dead   drives me to the end above a forest sky
    it is   deepening the white plague with its eyes

    this year   always the only year

it digs even emptier vision   is when waves smell each other's fetid genitals
it experiences a terminus   is on the height kept by seabirds
it collapses   is in sunlight ignorant of collapse

    it is being leaked away   the only ocean between me and who
    it is thinking   reverse blood's circulation
    a bug's broken-up bones   make a situation under the thumb
    bell ringing   just like struggling for life

it is the year   charging down at itself on an ever-faster sledge
it is the year   designating the loneliness of flesh
it is the year   separating our death in dead silence

it's really the unseen   that endlessly closes in under a piece of skin
it's really the sea   that madly shines in a lamp
    it is rewriting   on the face   lifelike   traces of ebbtide

JANUARY OF THE LIVING

    reality is a lie   yet now   loneliness is like a rat biting into my joints
    a room so dark that it's threatening
rock   sweeps away thirty moons carved on the ground

    still cannot clear   veins   all the while sounding the alarm
    what's the point of windows   when guts are nailed home
    death   striving to recall the sky

thirty rocky moons   prove that man is lightless

    lips that fear cold kneel to warm themselves
    clouds that fear memory   delete the steamed eyes
    fearing trees might empty   naked birds on branches don't fear every day
    fear   the reason I endure

rock   fixed in destruction   thirty drops of semen spurt out
dead fish overflow from thirty black moles on its own body
thirty faces   constitute a null time

    sailing   a room so big I have nowhere to disappear
    salt waking in boiled water from memory writing
    a dictionary of night   not missing any single year
each year   the preserved paediatrician in thirty kinds of moonlight
    snow-white nightmare looks up the islands in its embrace

    in untrue morning   so truly envy the funeral

SCHLOSS SOLITUDE

sea and sea flooding between windowsill and windowsill

sea and sea   falling   big snowdrift hand hides the wailing

    soundless   then determine we
    are humanity-less   underground garden squanders the seasons on our face
    bright red cement of flesh   the more motley it is
    the more an apple tree dying at both ends of the year grips fantasy
a head posted by grave and grave
the bluer it is   oozes thought's impure beauty

light and light flooding this lightless moment
    a twelve month field   slips past the ear like language
    twelve kinds of self-reaping harvests move into refrigerated sky
    twelve performances   all who come are the vanished
stone and stone fabricate our
essential   yielding beauty

    butterfly   embedded into the door makes a last dash every night
    on tongue tip   the world is as useless as a golden earlobe

flow away and flow away   and lamplight
    crowding behind a glass cliff
no flow   unwittingly butchered by peeping time
    too dangerous   ghosts and water one year older each day
too beautiful   go down a staircase that screams of tourists a century off

MIDNIGHT LETTER

leaving is a terrible mistake   not leaving is too
harbour   pruned to be the brightest day
road   aroused again by birds into early morning sex
you   hug death like a child

in sunlight's cruel project   we cannot leave this midnight

yet you left   two rock letter pages grip the instant of weighing anchor
flesh is a furious shore
whoever   hears whoever's rotting waves

a poem not yet finished   like a reef of little virgins
a fit of seagull screaming   still remembers us
remember   wings   curve in womb   so ignorant
still have never soared   soar out of   this brightest roe-coloured sky

this darkest   that no one can leave   not belonging to any single day
so you're still bound on bed   helpless to miss your own limbs
hearing a rudder   insert into a lie
hear a lie   widen a distance still widening after death
leaving   the blood-red timepiece of the guts calibrates pain
not leaving   smell each other's deep fiery skin more abstract than zero
no naked bodies do not strip naked into words

let thought then be what's after the end   blue is the mileage
kissing is the absence   broad day the midnight   then try silence again

THE TRANSMIGRATION OF GARDENS

weariest of spring are flowers   the gardener of death
polishing again   father   a cage releasing bright-coloured beasts
    one year   testicles hanging on blood-vessel branches allow wind to knead
    pomegranates   a piece of human skin is torn by the stupid wintering tailor
    wire mesh of grapes
    rusty teeth   bite with care a clitoris newly able to blush
spring   the studs on soles stuck with mince
each entrance even wetter than miscarriage
    father   what waters us is brine

    a set of six-year-old tiny shoulder-blades in the bath is a concept
    girl gazes from behind the eyes
    world   behind world

gather the bitterest moments   again remember living
on ocean's map   marbles secretly constructed like revenge
person singular neglected like a lover by the snowdrift sentences
everywhere tender green little thumbs   pop out again like they'd never been smashed
    this bottomless coffin   why does the scent of flowers never change
    the weariest of spring is to imagine

one year   that rocks can't borrow   that is familiar with each wave

    in father's garden   the dead have never increased
    this indigenous plot of the body   has never refused us another budding
    looked after by death   left behind by death

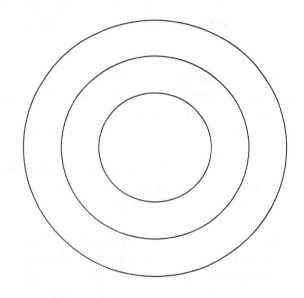

I. FEATHER DOOR

because of the failure to see   see again
because of nowhere   the flying flesh
the clouds above a criminal meadow
caress an address again

first room. hand on the moist wall, I walk down the stone staircase. darkness, another wall. the hanging marsh sucks in my fingers. arms, half a face, a beam of phosphorescence on the edge of a shoulder. darkness, this is how it reminds me: after all, one person is not dark enough; with no one, there isn't even a way of fighting to get darkness. I'm not just a body, but a voice. not just a voice but also the danger of stepping on every empty stair. here, I touch a feather door –

seek for this cemetery   then war pervades May
a madly barking dog   discerns the goodwill of the rotting map
white bones slowly stick out of the bird's head
birdsong   seeking the marble slab that withholds thought
    time emphasises this illness
    sit down   is age after age ruminating on the dark green sitters
    lullaby storm in the nostrils destroys another pram
    and mother   loses to this word mother

the smell of the dead's saliva in honey, and the smell of preservatives firmly stuck to feathers. a greyish white plastic blood vessel opens a darkroom of birds. let me touch, heart beating, on the door. the door's huge wings stick to my sense of touch. the sky, it's stuck in every flap of the wings. I listen, what stings the stillness on the four walls is nothing else, is precisely an ear drum. my, hands, they're chased at and pecked at by clusters of terrified fragments, dried up and pulled up, representing how many dead birds? how many dead birds, how many worlds? in, the infinity quietly secreted by a hollow feather –

May   mandible   false teeth   left knee   pubic hair   toes
May   cataracts   cartilage   kidneys   vocal cord   anus
May   navel-ring   crystal tongue   lung-lobed pelargonium
sunlight spewed over the ground   swans   tomb   who's May   wreckage
    the spectating city stuck on a beer-dirtied index finger
    scissors have cut close to the organ

play   then death comes endlessly near
the scent-spilling script of the dead is rehearsing

a porcelain bowl brim-full of pure water resonates. a boy holding a little hammer, startles a xylophone awake: is it true that each sound has at least three colours? child staring at darkness, knows nothing of darkness. eyes, they're more like the blind than eyelessness: is it true that we've been expelled by the flames in a room? three hours, reality, is installed into my body. the feather door sweeps me away, with flesh, and deep thought blaspheming against itself on an ugly stool: is it true that loss is also an aim –

because of the situation   no one ever escapes
wind stitches between the bone-gardens
feather cushion transplanted into the mouth of an earthen nurse
graveyard blue waving its hand
    because nothing is here
    cancel a journey again

this door implants itself into man-made night. a finger locks out a feather-whirling world. a kind of pain locks in the feather-whirling finger. is it true, angels exist at this time then? when a darker lesson is urging, when a madman again denies his own age –

May squeezes out a drop of butchering blood in mother's breast
rumbling thunder that shreds feathers
door-knocking on someone's forehead

II. RONDO AND COUNTERPOINT

this summer goes on   in the tiger leaves of Virginia creepers
a flock of tigers climb up a face
tiger skin covering the face
has only the look of acceptance
stone sex catches sunflowers over the hills and far away
stone-built courtyard stamped with tiger claws of starlight
jump into a girl's embrace   can't carve face or screams
this summer standing   resplendent   repeating

Mont Ventoux is in Provence in southern France. Viewed from far away, the summit in all seasons is an expanse of silvery white. But from close up, you will find it is not a snowcap, but heaps of crushed stones. In severe cold and violent winds, not a blade of grass grows. The peak, at a height of over two thousand metres, looks down over this land of wine, sunlight and romance.

Petrarch, when he wandered around here, was already famous in Europe for his sonnets. That night, what sort of pain made him feel the threat of the mountain closing in? How could he bear the speechlessness of these stones? Candlelight, borrowing perhaps a puzzled glimpse from the mirror, reflected a face he could not recognise, a face paler than moonlit rock. Cold, and it assailed his fingers. No one knew how horrible was the night he had passed through. The next morning, he left without bidding farewell. On the table, there was the first pure landscape poem in European history. Him, the first man to see this mountain.

twilight practising the void
on a printed portrait
fire is not vegetarian
fire eats those with faces
perfect disgrace is like something natural
printing ink boiled in dark blue
an oyster   a letter whose organs are read
practise a bright   null origin

A travel brochure on Banpo Prehistoric Village in Xi'an reads, 'The grave-yard lies to the north of the village. The heads of the dead all point to the west.'

The north, the only side where the sun never passes. Westward, where another dark night comes down from the hill. With a crash, an earthenware basin was broken, and the crowd in white hemp mourning clothes began to undulate. Wailing, it followed at my back, closely following this coffin. Six of us, at arm's length from each other, carried that one on our shoulders, the bones hitting the wooden planks with a rat-a-tat-tat. As soon as the coffin was nailed up, I had forgotten that face, forgetting how he tore at and devoured the bloody flesh of wild boars. All we did was to carry him, cursing the weight of the corpse while we thought about our meal after work. To the north, through the wood, let him fall into the coffin pit, his head pointing west.

In 1977, during the Cultural Revolution, I left the village where I had been sent to live and work with others in a production team. Six thousand years ago, in the Neolithic period, the inhabitants of Banpo did not record who the mourners were.

> the dull red flower buds screaming on flesh-coloured branches
> haven't slept all night   appreciating
> the double art of living and rotting
> my arm is a piece of work
> allowing you to compose
> field   though cultivated no springs have been dug
> springs everywhere but none have overflowed
> flow   still no better than the unique perfume of snake venom

When Brecht died, he was already an illustrious name in theatre history. His funeral was of course grand and solemn. People more ready to be responsible to the dead constructed, according to his will, a museum at his former residence: the address of the graveyard was chosen by himself, and it was separated from his former residence by only a wall. In winter evenings, standing in front of the gravestone, we can clearly see the lamplight from his study on the first floor. Branches hang dark above the snow. Footprints to and fro cover a path lined with holly.

Years passed. People were wondering about the great playwright's last work. He sat by the window every day. The window, like another blank sheet of paper, exactly the same as the one on the writing desk. Messengers sent by the theatre to enquire returned empty-handed as always, all of them repeating what he muttered to himself, 'What play is unique? A play which is unique to each person?'

His will was found under a pile of paper ash cremated with meticulous care.

> hungry reflection in a pigeon's pupil
> balances the broadened water surface

the deck unfolds a farewell landscape
blood travels against the motion of light
renewing the fish in dark waves
an instant   a brown rock's wake
so resplendent under the threat of birdsong
keeping watch   on the sky's far away details

The recollection of a fiction: Bergamo, a small hill town dating from ancient Roman times, has a beautiful city wall and is built in typical medieval style. From Lecco by Lake Como, forty minutes by local train will get you there.

Agnello D'Oro Hotel is situated behind the cathedral. When the church bells chime, you are both transformed by the chimes into a stream of light, flying, like a flock of swallows long used to this racket, above the dull red and light grey tiles lining the roofs. The streets, below. On the square, the café named after the poet is as usual, full. You both remember, the marble there seems to have been hacked out. For hundreds of years, gentle fingers have been enough to inspire fear in the rock. Gentle caresses fall on that nakedness like strokes of a whip. You remember, behind the tightly shut venetian blinds, some bodies are exhibiting their own incomplete beauty to each other. Remember, demand once again, come once again. Bergamo was flattened long ago.

even wasps cannot
wound is   word is
that which is twisted off dead sunflowers
plump and strapping is   stuttering
golden electric wire netting
the mouthless passion of mines in water
an insulating head is stung
if   I can still create a lie

Walk alongside a railway and you will suddenly be there: the two Berlins that confront each other in silence end abruptly here. The Berlin Wall, after it was pulled down, broken up and sold off in tiny bits as tourist souvenirs, there were two parallel lines left over. Extending. The green grass, looking as if it is painted on the ground, is much too quiet; the dead strip of these years is too narrow. Except for a few trees which didn't get around to growing tall and which remind you of the vastness of it, you can hardly believe so many ghosts could be locked up in there.

Schweigen in German refers exclusively to 'reticence'. It is different from 'silence' in English, which can also mean 'stillness'. I did not continue a proposed dialogue on the topic of reticence with the poet Uwe Kolbe, an East German by birth. Not because someone stopped us, but 'reticence' demanded it – listen. Listen to it: that which denies language, that which is not even wordlessness, endlessly deepening under a throat, deep down at the level of confirming a mouth, of confirming the death chamber with the electric chair. It is in there, it is always more than the opposite of sound, that which compels us to ask ourselves continuously, 'No?'

No – if you cannot hear, between two invisible walls, the pain that ghosts are still powerless to surpass.

    hope so much this is just a vain throw
    red or green   ball
    thrown to whom   baby rolling
    death's inspiration accurately
    thrown at a cooked apple on the branch
    golden   hanging in the direction you want to go
    giving you a reason for deciding not to go
    to betray your own   painful orbit

There should be a graveyard for the war dead here, or so at least the London map says. Here, apart from the indifferent backs of alleys, there's only this park. May pushes the war farther and farther away. Under the noon sun, a pram sits quiet. A young mother opens a book in her lap. A little farther away, a few high school students are practising goal kicks in front of a temporary goal of schoolbags. Birdsong, bright and abstract, seems like part of the sky. This is a May when even dogs are too tired to roar at strangers. On my way here I asked one person after another, along the path by the brook. No one knows this graveyard. It seems to have disappeared behind Spring. I've got nothing written in my notebook, so I sit down, giving in to the absence – As the park is around me; the circular waves of London, are around the just-opened bottle of beer at the corner of my mouth.

    the stone reproduced by every hour
    is reproducing us
    four mushrooms on the decayed floor
    four roots penetrate the chessboard of death
    four limbs   kept in the mouth
    fingernails hotly pinch
    this weakness   this work
    this room   this earth   this universe

An artist's face is carved by his art. A late photo of Ezra Pound, and the *Cantos* – which created which? Are the lines of his poems all wrinkled? Or does his expression look like it has been cut by glaciers? In the end, to read the face and to read the texts are one and the same. Pound's face gathers together a life's risk, pride, and failure in poetry. He hated hospitals and mirrors.

Another man who is the enemy of time: he casually kneads time's clay into labyrinths, gardens and tigers; yet he never understood how the darkness in his body came about. Did the danger of becoming a blind man make him talk about time? Or did the talk of time render him blind? No matter. In short, one day, he accepted it – in the world that leans on his walking stick there are tenses no more, just like there are no tenses in the square black shapes of Chinese verbs. Everything is situation, between the search for a word in an oral account and a murder on an indistinct ceiling; between the attempt to grope for the armrest of a sofa and the Great Wall built by the First Emperor of China.

He is one of those few people who live in null time. The darkness handed down through six generations gave him wisdom. But, did he regret it? – 'Tell me, what is my face like?' Eighty years old, the excessively youthful face had already been crumpled by memory. An excessively vicious joke? So, he writes mirrors. The terror of a flat icy sheet. A face that fails to see finally becomes a mirror of time. What he touches is empty inside.

Jorge Luis Borges did not understand Chinese.

a tiger jumps out from a birthday
Sunday is inspecting a stone carving
jerk-off trees deeply love queues
this summer deeply loves a damp axe
endlessly hacking an armpit
smells   how man is despised
this sunlight scrapes vision clean on green leaves
nobody can escape from a cool shady poem

Ban-Goo read out these Wordes by Candle-light: 'This age hath no Heröes, and even a simple Ninny might acquire Greatnesse.'

Ban-Goo said thus unto himselfe: 'The *First Emperor* seized on the Six King-doms, built the Great Wall, decreed the Axel-tree and the Letters, burned the Bookes and buried the Scholars alive. But all his overswaying Authoritie could no-whit help when, after his death, the Captaine *Shang-Yoo* burned the Palace of Ah-Fang and all the Countrie three hundred miles about. And *Shang-Yoo* afterward cut his Throate on the banks of the Woo-Jang, when the Commoner

Lew-Bang altogether overthrew him. Can this truly bee my Chronicle of Han?'

And *Ban-Goo* recounted how *Shang-Yoo* digged out the *First Emperors* greate Tombe, stole all its Treasures away, and set fire to that under-grounde Palace. Thankes therefore bee to his famous Chronicle of Han, that the massy Pile of yellow Earthe beneath Black-Horse Hill in *Shan-Shee* hath remained more than two thousand yeares inviolate, for no man thought to unburie his Histories.

Had this age then no Heröes? Verily, more than two thousand yeares after, men speake yet of Imperial Historian *Ban Goo*'s most excellent Lies.

III. CAPELLA TOWER

destruction is our knowledge   but this condemned tower
whose mouth   whose eyes brimming with pitch
hasn't yet reached that wordlessness

    a graveyard is part of the dead's bloodstain
    May   part of the graveyard

light, is so formed. no one sees it. in the feather door, no one knows, on this
pitch-black floor, light is secretly drawing its concentric circles –

room   deadly poisonous knowledge in four walls
a twisted and broken tongue in the keyhole
flesh   the knowledge of getting lost
smells   worst possible news just posted missing from someone else

    as a look into the distance   is made into part of blindness

no curse that isn't burning. no field of white snow, that doesn't come from
omnipresent underground sight. dead fish leaping and diving in an electric
ocean, always with its silver, serving as a foil to the all-night gliding seagull.
nothing, that doesn't ooze drop by drop from the darkness of my bone marrow –

    sacrificers   part of blades of grass printed with a human face
    sky   part of motley green rust on the carved wing
ghosts still arrive on time
conceive of a bed   this night broken into fragments
wake skin   a starlight dictionary
when reciting the personless   distinct footsteps on crushed stones

    let us hear and understand our own fear

    a windproof body   a room's darkest part

in the fantasy of the camera lens, a person is nothing but feet, legs and an
unrecognisable face. the radius of light, it turns darkness into substance; nothing
but a glass teardrop hanging at the end of a power cable, confirming that the
punishment for language, it continues in silence too; nothing but light not
letting anybody off, tightening its ligature again and again –

spring inverted outside the window   like a dry azure well
tower   looks deep down into the depths of miscarriage
a field's old gramophone record under the plough again
a book of dusk speeds up its growth into something soon to be harvested
a skein of snowstorms impatient to scald to death lovers rising from the horizon

twelve months following the bloodstained rut of a month
war has to transmigrate inside one person
the dumb are more confused   more crazy   than words

a concentric circle is all. in the feather door, the sound of light's curse, echoes of countless wrecked yesterdays. in each sound, there's a wrecked self. we're thousands of years apart, and must share a dark side. the inner side. let those who have lived, and those who are living lean together with their own fetid reek, so as to bear a reality no greater than a single word.

but even curses   are powerless to stop

gravestone   fits into the lightest part of weathered names
lighter still   in the ocean's shadow a room is moving
more perfumed still   in wild pigeon pitch the sunlight is dazzling
no one powerful enough to destroy this tower twice
dawn   ghosts write out birdsong
every pine needle's green copied again
glaring again   at the nominal white in a sheep's eye
no memory harsher than the exam of a whole life breathing

in a room's shadow   an ocean is moving

we're formed this way: condemned – as broken walls and fences, we face the collapse and collapse of every white sheet of paper; as words, we're expelled into silence, by what we wrote ourselves; as absence, we have no choice, on a footstool, to be locked up by a photo of the dearly departed, in Babylon's foundation that is made of flesh –

die once again   still part of death
light   a part that makes the effort to reach a dark maximum

destruction   goes on constructing this tower
knowledge of language forsaken   white bones united in a poem

knowledge of vision deleted   design eye-
sockets as a hatred-nursing   non-sleeping map
ghosts   midnight unchanged inside their eyes   breast feed
reflected in such an old mirror of a baby   mirror with a faraway flowing face
    the height we reach   is where we fall

    moved once again by an ancient betrayal

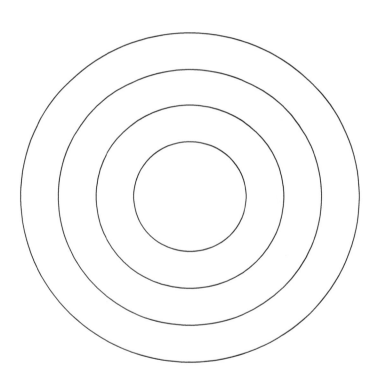

CONSTRUCTED GROUND

the garden is only at the foot of the cliff   extinct volcano
threatening the ocean for a whole year
it's you walking down the street   it's street turned into bridge
under the bridge corpses wrap a tediously long rainy season
it's Auckland that polished the bloody axe bright in seagulls' screaming

it's Sydney hanging beneath an oyster balcony
passing drunkards in the dusk mumbling to themselves again
yellow waves of jaundice   break into a basket of ripened apples
it's New York auctioned off to the festering yellow snow

stray cats   taxi drivers disappear into the alleys of Paris or Prague
rancid smells   gush out of the bowels of Vienna and Los Angeles
it's a Brooklyn basement on a madman's seabed
counting the sand leaking down

flocks of concrete birds   cover your timeless window
it's Berlin on its sleigh always sliding to midnight
waxed street light   glowing earlier still in blood vessels
a pearl among mossy eyelids
it's what is watched   watching you rush to the destruction ground

the chime is only at the foot of the cliff   fondly injuring drowned hearing
cliff   tumbles into London sky
flowers at the funeral grip a face through four seasons
thorn of grammar   pricks newspaper headlines below silver fish-scales
is the river that threatens poets minting another marble pillow
breathing conceals a city in the abstract sound of rain
you're unmoving   two parallel ranks of gravestones blindly passing

it's   this place that never changes
only then does one collect the disaster of one's own past

REPEATED COMEDY

lovers' flesh always picks on peeled-off paint
but logs of the dead are nailed together for a floor
in new year's nail hole   doomsday is a fire escape

come out of laughter and then there's the ocean
escape over the ocean's cliffs and then there's the dining table
immigrants sleepwalk from the dining table   each a blood-red passport

in a lovers' nail hole doomsday is a blood-stained passport
to come out of laughter is a fire escape
you   chosen by the deathbed to face night all alone

all stories are set in the corners of false teeth
the you of the story's setting had resin all over your body
boys all foolishly burning at the crossroads

degeneracy has the sweet distance of putrescence
when pears are hung on windows   passion under the moonlight can't be refused
hands that thirst for pain   can't push away the ocean's fetters

when all stories rot away and are nailed together for the ocean's fetters
degeneracy   like moonlight foolishly burning
your bed   changed again but still under the sky's avalanche

move into March   green grass grows from wild doves' eyes
August   heavy rain filling graves drowns the dead again
November branch tip   the last apple of each year

use a lover's mouth till it's even older
a throat that gulps down endings   disdains to make up lies
tongue's slide just there for a pile of white crap to fall deeper down

lies of March fall deeper down
throat   is drowned every time to come out of laughter
your sleep   strips away your flesh into blankness

finally settling down in a bedroom is betrayal   no more no less
anaesthetising once   excises countless anaesthetised bodies
life   becomes   the wreckage of death

come out of blood-stained passports   accept what you can't endure
come out of the new year   swallow what you've just spewed on the ground
from doomsday   to another shame-squandering doomsday

you can't come out of a bedroom because you've locked the fire escape
nail in   the existence of a nail hole
to wildly hope   don't be woken by tinnitus

A LABYRINTH GRADUALLY GROWING

– infinity of fallen leaves rustling, rustling
Du Fu (712-770)

the mirror has lost its reflection from too much description of it
snowdrifts in the mirror   whitewash the quiet myths on four walls
the white of skeletons never fabricates elsewhere
                    I ooze out of here
    listen to the sound of cars cutting a morning LP
    mist   licks across the wet wings of dead birds on a billboard
    mother lion sleeping all night in a rubbish heap
    listlessly chews her contempt for humans again

mirror becomes weary of
the illusion of neighbours washing each other
    a street sucks nothingness from the tip of a frozen red little thumb
    curl up in the rain and look down at buses far away
    lung dancing in flu music
    coughing   the naked ghosts under an occasional ray of sunlight
    heating wrung to its weakest is highlighting a cold home
                I'm paralysed in here

who is whose mirror   a corridor like the world too long to be walked through
from all the houses a window sees the ocean off
death   a wall hung with photos of the dead
change   only then can be completely changeless
    at mother's sick corner a bundle of fiery red silvergrass
    closing in on the boy who illuminates evil
    hide behind a door   yet you're still on the spot
    lamplight catches up with   a yolky mud eyeball in camphor's medicinal smell
    deleted   this only spot

                as far away as skin
                I learn painlessness from myself
                listen intently to a drop of blood that can't flow
mercury   collapses when it's riveted
speaks while collapsing   finds after speaking the crowd out

the shape that I rent to this address
house moves into the name   visiting clouds move into an afternoon
fallen leaves   are all infinite

here   mirror in its silent centre
here   I am my own far away

A LABYRINTH GRADUALLY GROWING

– ceaseless river waves rolling, rolling
Du Fu

days bring death   or death has revealed the days
this is again that day   drenched roof turns black
marble rusts   in a blaze someone crosses this night of their own
        so we have arrived
  the past   on the bed a puddle of chalk flooded with your sex
  plastic baby spiders are climbing trees
  vainly hoping nipples a pair of candles melted a thousand years
  more passionate than the sky about being burnt red   being hung

moment of darkness   or the darkness expressed by the moment
we have arrived   dismantled bones
  affirm   what a saw repeatedly memorises
  your naked book   climbs teeth
  tears' soft ladder is climbing the blankness at the bottom of the eyes
  the placenta of tonight   affirming
  moment necessary for the worst news   pain   affirms time's root
        how much harm can we still store

this is again a night when arms stretch to the fireplace
bright golden tongues   knotted by the sound of wind
glass trembles   endless biographies of dark clouds
man sits into past events   or wild beasts of past events catch up with man
  shattered as the past   or ruthlessly shattered by the past from within
  rainy seasons of a thousand years take you for their direction
  no more fear   a green tender leaf in dark grey concrete wings
  group sex abandons a face
  history mops up assumptions and is sintered into a horrible ejaculation

        our tiny throats
        blocked into   a much too late cry for help
        are flung onto the wall
affirm   under the transparent skin there's only the past
whoever arrives at his own impossible then no longer passes

limited in the only death
you use the colour of flesh to condense the ocean's hunger
waves   are imagining

this moment   the fact of miscarriage
the killing floor has arrived   none of the dead will resist

A LABYRINTH GRADUALLY GROWING

– constantly travelling a million miles of autumn melancholy
Du Fu

city probes lyric posture   redresses a drop of blood
parallel sunlight on onions and a postman's uniform
city is immortal   like everyone's tiny reality
    those space-walks
 walking at home   an iron fire-ladder droops its ears
 half past eight   terrorists bomb breakfast breadcrumbs on time
 half past twelve   a spastic alarm clock reverberates in the stomach
 seven in the evening   a silver airplane shines like a drunken brooch

sink deeply into a stretch of blue   city's daily rhetoric
the pitch-dark doorway between sheets and blankets
 the gilding heel of a shoe forgets that it's an island itself
 in spring's single eye ten thousand peach blossoms go in and out
 a bridge over the remains of afternoon tea
 a condom filled with water dangles from a boy's mouth
 bronze tellers' faces full of seagull-shit mottoes
    those giggles   make a date with cheap rain

they select from junk shops sentences older than themselves
your wind whistles through vertebra clothes racks
we neatly lick   on the hangnails of fishhooks
the emotionless existence of a transparent jawbone
 a milligram of darkness in the second's moving tip
 stars stabbing into age shine with what electric current   what tranquilliser
 what erudition leaves her naked to the sleeping vagina
 one at night   two legs of the horizon are close enough to grip me in between
 three in the morning   sperm living in damp furrows are reciting epics

    those application forms   IOUs   account books
    angel tax   vet food
    prudent lives
city uses the hose of blood vessels   rinse
now   the noun that lifts window gauze in wards

how many skulls create an oil stain on the pillow in a small hotel
the glamour that life cannot postpone
turning dreamlessness into power

stop   elegant zero   acme of style
driving to the harbour of heaven

A LABYRINTH GRADUALLY GROWING

– mounting this balcony alone in years of sickness

Du Fu

denying oneself is denying a time   a place
denying this place isn't Du Fu's cottage   forty-two years old
Holmleigh Road in the Tang dynasty
                    denying   the distance from madness to madness
   poets   desperate teaching material for each other
   this sweating of mother's demolishes the roof
   gives birth to Sunday's chime
   hands covered with snails after rain   grope in the post-mortem peril of the sea
      sea skins and mounts the white bones

a piece of porcelain drifts in a bird's orbits
denying a stony balcony isn't rapidly flowing
   poetry   desperate teaching material for poets
   bodies making love on a lawn make us ogle as we avoid them
   war   twitches like the flowers under scissors
   a boat of refugees drives out of a withered womb
   a red chimney has registered all the man-made storms in sky
                    deny   so you've already admitted

no thing that isn't a crime preserved by babies
no time that isn't psychology soaked with salt
no address   can separate universally present migraine
lean toward   at forty-two   a tree outside the window that doesn't deny refusal
   so walk into a Tang dynasty that bursts forth in white flowers on street corners
   so drink a drop of London water seven times excreted before it reaches the sea
   press the fingerprints of death
   press to ring   March's only doorbell
   heavy camouflage net of leaves hears a corpse pull apart the foreign soil

                    deny   each native place that chokes to death in poetry
                    from self to self
                    don't deny the character of destruction
no face can deny   the upper reaches of a toadstool
thinking drills holes in a silver skull

68

being flooded implies a mouthful of wine on the stairs
being remembered by a biography writer a thousand years ago implies
writing   has written our sickness down

a mirror losing its reflection   forever re-grows its flesh
and forever   means never

REPEATED GROUND

you bite   a blood-red cobweb inside your body
you're more careful than spiders
biting invisible details in the dark

yesterday always lacks a drop of fixing solution
nostrils smell   sunlight going far away in the texture of old clothes
a memoir accumulates the poison of time

you bite   a spider caught in blood-red cobwebs
so warm living among the dead
a needle from the old days sews the sallow ashes of mothers' bones

so like the moonlight   you're more careful than spiders
chew the wordless chapter of a hospital
the dead know the position of absence can't be given up

a memoir accumulates the poison of time
the sunlight   the farther off the more conspicuous
details of a poisonous writer in darkness
spiders   the story of spider remorse

this morning a burst of birdsong
links to that person tied up and forgotten in a marsh
torn down alive by mosquitoes in a night

the sallow consanguinity that mothers vomit goes on being pregnant
so warm living among the dead   honey of old ballads
collecting the miserable shrieks of your memories of being loved

so like the cheering of children flinging a cat on the wall   the dead know
on an greasy rope   your remains tempt you to crawl nearer
spiders pounce on the future with cut-down tiger claws

CONSTRUCTED COMEDY

the dead know this position is absent and can't be given up

at the foot of the cliff   tender green leaves open a gilded chair
in a garden   man sits and strips the names off
a piece of snow-white fat sits and strips man off

football   spring's blind spot

the dead know
in snow-white fat sits the putrescent fear of dirt
                    the 7-character line unfolds
                    a situation of general cleaning up

four limbs are still like a platform
from mud's mercerised pyjamas a female collarbone still protrudes
garbage bags still hang on the pear tree flutter and whine like kites
still   madly long for another way of life

nostrils   turn the bright blue rifling of a gun's bore
cemetery   shows a row of ancient blanks
lying under the sunlight of a dead sky

                    the 7-character line unfolds
                    a form of vanishing

accepting   a canal of food that washes away the countless scarlet lips
caressing   the bed-rearing wasps that sting the masturbators
forgiving   a basin of bathwater where sperm is scalded to death
only at the foot of the cliff are gales   scraping away parallel sense organs
                    seven horizons
                    define seven kinds of forgetting

even more deaths still can't complete one judgment day
even more mince still not enough to fill the desires gobbled by an address
ten thousand rainy nights still won't overflow this wrongly written rainy night

not person-less   only non-person singular

rotting dread of dirt brushes with all its might the loneliness of a public toilet
the garden transported away again by a flame-red public bus
every flesh-coloured living leather suitcase   pours once again
the knowledge of death
poisoned four seasons originate once again

                         the 7-character line   this starlit sky
                         struggles free of time absolutely

a football skull endlessly kicked into the transparent emptiness of space

no such position even at the foot of the cliff
the cliff of snow-white fat   even without an end
an ocean swum across has never used a tiny bird's head to gather light years
reiterate   the adversity of being picked up

not a character unfamiliar
this characterlessness   breaks five pictographed fingers

the dead know   the way   no one has a chance to leave

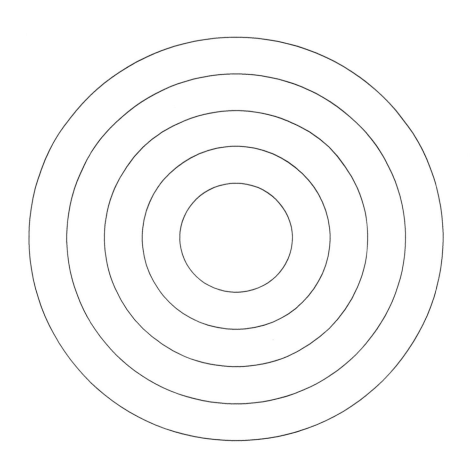

言

TALKING

TALKING 言

a wrist watch dug up from the ground ticks away
wrist   vanishes
is timed

foreign trademarks on trainers
empty out toes

walk   into   a drop of blood

out   dripping   tick   tock

being killed exchanged decomposition

clay   smile
poppy   black red plump
bullet holes   oysterses

embrace Braille
raise   a touching spider

drip   tock

an even softer little brush can't wake
the sleeping sex sunk deep in each other

bring the time of us
time that the battery stammers
the other side   green radium light dazzles

arrive

unearthed
gliding black birds

archaeology of the now

SWAY 誰

yank so yeah you chin
fen sought bam show shin
choose ewe add fling sin
moat high ease door fin
eik wall gun gog

sigh you anti dan
squeak couching ban
doe hay bushy shan
coolie herring fan
fizz way chaw cog

QUESTIONING 詰

whether or not   death is deep as a chamber's shape

is the rainstorm of children driven again into the corner of flesh?

who rehearses cruelty on a piano?

revising   brutish ocean of tiny syllables

why do children conduct the brightly coloured age that is an avalanche?

whether   music turns humans into a foreign language

or not   window pauses   halting into sunlight's deathly pale frequency

where   which hand writes down the nursery on fire in the sky

page of sheet music   how does it demolish everything daily

five fingers   how do they lock composers in

what can a room hear   in children's pitch-dark centres

who   mad   ly   de   sires   to   ap   proach   ze   ro?

weakest   whether or not   deepest into a string's hidden pain

ink wash sky   dead children run   dis   tance

LIES 謊

beauty sans home
beauty sans   home   sans its
colour   sans home may   Homeward Ho!   say
yellow red blue white black their rūpa vedanā samjña samskāra vijñāra
score pound foot shoal pint flock sheet leaf brace volume gaggle fathom dram
super al con ician mono ante ism per inity alysis cata intra ana ness pro ation ery
say hit drink play smile eat touch shoot fly co-in-cide pisc-itate hypno-tise
dying   attending to clarifying the foam on a glass of beer
stone borrows   masked experience
home   sans   its   beauty
is true

OBITUARY 訃

this date is translated into our flesh and blood
chorusing fingertips
excavated music

concert   confirms ears
full moon   confirms
no performance not undressed   unroofed

cutting out the eyelids of stars

pink ribs
resonate   black

this date punishes the day that doesn't exist
a translation carefully listens
that vanished   that never pain-abandoning

that collective   left leg

throat
recollects

tenses of facial expressions
illuminate   our   flower   pond
the other side   green radium light dazzles

so many

deaths   powerless to overstep a number

syllables

both delving hands hold maggots
wriggling   synopsis of man

passing

confirming   there's no past
the same side   musical instruments clapping
a storm speeding up to pass through concrete

TROPOS PRŌTOS PHŌTOS NOESIS EPOS LOGOS ANTHRŌPOS GNOSIS

ANTHROPHOTOS PROTO

POETRY 詩

zero
    date stops at a dangerous moment
translates as
    art of losing blood from a tiny heart
boundaries between drop and drop of water
    likened to history
the edge of bird call
    Dante lies in Ravenna
the place where clouds originate
    disinterred wristwatch worn on a Sarajevo street
plural darknesses
    children compose music
gap between the winds
    red marble sliced up
pain grasping the hands
    dusk   withdraws from windows
leaves   nibbling their own green
    shoot autumn's building in the back
linguistics
    accommodates reality
tongues of fire
    licking the vital part of love
one internal secretion   we're tottering
    Dante   his back covered with the bullet holes of children's voices
lying at the bottom of sea
    be the reader of the orchestra of execution
by zero turned into
    what looks like a zero   an obscure forefinger points to Chinese
            this second   what isn't poetry

土

EARTH

EARTH 土

death   reduces repetitions to once
last night stormy
sinking into twelve mirrors
a meadow wipes these sentences clean

swans   a snowy white library
twelve catalogues stroll past
in the female silver bottles
moonlight   roaring waves

you can't not watch
the golden afternoon nap in eyes of mother-of-pearl
September inscribed with words   deep as a face
talk   then you have to exist

beneath the feet   a soundproof bedroom opens wide
twelve ends reflect visitors
a crystal zoo
from a faraway interstellar whisper

the necessary once
at least   in the mirror
the upside-down gods
without your dim flesh and blood

ALTAR 壇

a thought cuts up the floor
the electric saw   echoes your palm-embedded
sunlight

a golden cathedral
sliding horizontally
the time you create   a piece of white china

summer embedded into a track of flesh
the bitter smell of men in abandoned barracks
the dead bell couldn't wake up   the little town's drowsiness

wheat fields move into windows
the horizon highlights your blackening rhythm
a revolution lacquered purple

an ear-piercing god twisted tight at the other end of a wire
geometry reinforcing shadows
living   known as

one   embedded into
any single line on the silk of a palm
creating its own doomsday

GAIA 坤

man is a sketch
the heartbeats of sand   a fatal dream
more reticent than a room
ocean leaks down along the beautiful waist of a glass
more ignorant than light   more like a single night than love

language gives you the theme
sand grips you in slow motion
a pair of tiny dancing breasts
deny dying in death
the more delicately a moment is depicted   the shorter it becomes

the more a bright window between the legs hears
a glass of wine next door
lies   teach you
create a dark truth in your own eyes
ocean's pattern placed above a non-human aim

more familiar with destruction than bird claws
in dreams   under golden skin a murmuring
grain of
unreachable by even the prettiest finger
sand

TOMB 塚

the quiet of the afternoon is like an empty space backstage
the calendar won't tell that capacity
a red ticket   sold
lets you interview your own shabby organs
smile   whitewashes a bombed-out city
blood possesses unrecognised speed
charging into the stony nerve of a flashgun
enlarging   the tunnel on one site

the funeral is only   part of beauty
bright enough like the corner of this afternoon
to exhibit your blankness
a part that even the gloaming can't heal
without the audience's applause   won
the flowers on a photo   which don't fear wear and tear
a myth has been terrifyingly corrected
the world   can't stand myths

PLACE 境

a little creature's teeth secretly sneer
plaster guesses your age

under the shadowless lamp of sunlight
flesh is a fall of white snow

snow-white renews pelvic flowers
plump clouds of hearts hang all round a room

vertebra wax
when is it fire when is it tears

what dream   is dreamed in the public eye
a bloody hook tempting sharks

the more incomplete you are
plaster   the truer to imagining

a surgical procedure subtracts a corpse into a crowd
a farewell   plagiarists fill the street

plaster   takes root
a trap between your breasts sums up the dark

no one betrays this notion
no destruction   hasn't been promised in advance

shape set   like this workshop
everyday   produces the same class of snow-white solids

RUINS 墟

weariness   has preserved a secret butterfly
you who sit by the twilight window
join the darkening view
a frostbitten pear
unfolds dark clouds   rams a tiny balcony
autumn's   expected revenge

keep far from   silver white stones water-softened at the station
the dead the only ones not to betray this poem
your   vineyard train
pulls out into the heavy terminus fog
the anchor of tonight weighed from a body
savouring   a sweet revenge

write from memory   the passion that can't go on collapsing
you are driven into this dead corner
a bridge   can't break what doesn't even have words
you whose darkness guarantees your placelessness
sit in here   wait till you get your own
long treasured-up revenge

POETRY 詩

zero
>   reduces death to the common once
repeats
>   the garden in the thoughts of the dead
subtracting the subject
>   subjecting a lawn of golden pubic hair to the mower
non-tense
>   onto spider-web of hair it flies
moves
>   lonely dog opera
moving
>   a child's immortal talent for trampling on a flower
weep   and so weep endlessly
>   the flagstone covering a poet's face
at the limitless
>   flings birds far out of a womb
madness   flings a madman away
>   you bury the mouth organ
garden
>   a drop of blindingly bright ink in the thought of the dead
completes
>   suturing
a
>   mother   ten thousand flesh roses make up
situation
>   not writing   already died together
everyone is an old work   smelling a rotten book jacket
>   repeating   the zero last night in mad imagining
>>   *no more possible*   then that's poetry

寸

INCH

INCH 寸

L for lamentation
once reined in   of   colour   sinking   pool
commemoration already not
dead horse or beauty's brow
wind   howling

TIME 時

disappearing or thinking   same direction

only   where   sunlight moving from the body
bell or nil   same thought   round
three years   now a thousand autumns
living not

only   commemoration turns into
where   agave fluttering in

GRAB 奪

the damaged one   so like
neck lovely as an unfinished verse
sky acting the blue foreground so much

moonlit palace in a feather's song
live or hate   both too tedious
even if neck lovely as
before the horses or on the slope
even if our own half-line   wakes in pain

stories   not by chance
G for
grace

YES 對

word were   jaded jade   sounded sound   rounded pound   leaned line
between   or premeditated absence
identical table
a cloud observing

word were   lying beneath a white porcelain brow

bells drench the rain   ghosts
no strength to go farther

commemoration   were once dead still not
sleepless horn playing
white bark were inexhaustible burning birds
three years already   ghost's thought
lamp turns its head

disappear   moon in eclipse

SHOOT 射

green   if it's not trees it's only eyes
love is

three years   a poem endlessly writing its own ending
until October implying

disappear   expose
piercing period pain of snow-bright windows
blindfolded river of sex   miserably dazzling
this word   bridge   pets our loveliest three years

look   hollow meaty clam of Valentine's Day

so twilight implies a kitchen yellow-lacquered
skirt can't change into its gold colour
in a small hotel a bed of lustful imagninings
                    in step with poetry
think until the end   until October
watch happiness come so simply
like fallen flowers   just blossomed in the eyes of the dead
like eyes and poems escaping

SEEK 尋

future　　strapped into bones like a function word
if only to delete a poem from reality

the imperial armies refuse to advance
beautie-browèd horses in martial attire ride to
a snowstorm of adjectives

a tree full of parking apples
even the emperor is baffled by archaeological nouns
drinking tea　　white paper slightly aged
　　　　　　　　seeming's
seem　　evening　　numerals are like reuniting fields
the old jeep of stars bounced by someone again
subtraction　　organises a lump of crystal between the trees
　　　　　　　　subtracted to more

of circles　　dark
of zero　　a broken neck
releases　　children

hope or inflammation　　the same electric bell rings through the classroom of flesh
country in a bottle or hibernation　　clot together into purple and brown
tongue　　drooping between two verbs
unmoving　　the sum of destruction has never been more than one person
　　　　　　　　returning

POETRY 詩

nil
        vanishing to three
word
        three autumns go over the border
far
        three times   toward the light birds radiate medicinal shadows
from
        Dante is the one refused by a key
it–
        vanishing is thought
self's
        what can't be redeemed   stows away to form the next line
own
        chorusing yellow-brown nothingness
past
        halting   dead hometown road pointed by rails
tale
        three chapters   three farthest clouds
con–
        secretion
firms
        fallen leaves   millions of scarlet polished fingernails
this
        slash the sheet music   existing has no lower limit
second
        vanishing into the beloved
poem
        post-mortem   beautiful story
is

Driving to the Harbour of Heaven:
translating Yang Lian's *Concentric Circles*

Concentric Circles is not an easy book, in any sense. It makes great demands on the reader in any language, and it has often been a vexing and frustrating experience attempting to translate it, though I must also say that Agnes Chan and I have just as often felt the exhilaration of rising to a challenge and the rewards that come when the puzzle of a recalcitrant text is finally unlocked.

Yang Lian has written to me that it is the 'most important piece since I came out from China', and that he intends the work to be seen as a matched pair with his book-length poem cycle *Yi*.[1] It is, he insists, emphatically not a political work, but instead an artistic work focused on 'deep reality'.[2]

Yang Lian's style, it seems to me, is one founded on a type of collage, where many small fragments, each complete in itself, are aligned together in a series of patterns to form a grander mosaic: from line to line, poem to poem, cycle to cycle, book to book, in ever-widening concentric structures. Like William Burroughs' cut-ups, they are startling and disjointed on one level while remaining coherent on another, but Yang Lian is collaging images, not words – "image cut-ups", perhaps. Each image remains self-sufficient and perfect, creating an extraordinary and vertiginous effect as the reader's focus is shifted willy-nilly from micro to macro, the eye and mind constantly jolted between different levels of reference and different levels of attention. There is order here, a precisely shaped and crafted order, as intricate as the work of the mosaic-builder or the watchmaker. Though they may be ambiguous, and though the meaning of each fragment is not always instantly obvious, his images are exact and true. A good example of this precision is in the opening lines of his poem cycle *Where the Sea Stands Still*:

> blue is always higher   just as your weariness has chosen
>   the sea   just as a man's gaze compels the sea
>   to be twice as desolate [3]

At first when I read these lines, I was paying more attention to the stanza as a whole, and, inasmuch as I gave much thought to it, I assumed 'blue is always higher' to be an abstract kind of thought, a ranking of the ocean's blue as having a higher, more abstract quality, with the added possibility of its referring also to the blue of the sky, which is positioned above the sea. Then in 2003, Yang and I were in Auckland for a poetry conference:[4] though he had lived in Auckland for several years – during the period when *Where the Sea Stands Still* was conceived – and I had visited the city a couple of times, we had never been there together. As we walked or drove around the city that week, Yang constantly drew my eye to small details in the cityscape or in the scenery, referring them to lines and images in his poetry. Finally, we were invited out to Mike Hanne's place, close to Karekare beach, where Jane Campion's *The Piano* was filmed. As we arrived, Yang rushed me out to the deck to look at the view: as we looked down the narrow valley to where the sea was framed between two almost perfect 45 degree hill slopes, the optical illusion that the blue seawater was rising away from us at a steep angle was near-perfect. 'That's it!' he said. 'That's where *blue is always higher!*' And it was, perfectly precise and physically present, there in front of me. Nothing abstract about it, but a deftly executed sketch of a physical phenomenon, inserted into a complex tesselation of images.

I will not speak here of the nature of the poetry – Yang Lian does this himself in his Preface to this book – but something must be said here about how the work of translation went on. Yang gave me the manuscript of *Concentric Circles* in late 1997, at a moment when I was overwhelmed with my teaching job, and little able to find time to take on a work of this complexity. However, even at first glance it was obvious that there were some very difficult problems, and some tricky poems that would be great fun to do, so I got into the habit of sitting down with it at odd moments, often with a beer or two after work, jotting down ideas as they came. My friends John Thor Ewing, Francis R. Jones and W.N. Herbert were often co-conspirators in the early stages of playing with rough drafts and making likely-looking fragments: I thank them here for their willingness to join in the fun. But by the end of 1999, when I left for Hong Kong, there was little of the book in English but a few fragments and sketches in pencil jottings on the facing pages of the manuscript. So it remained until 2001, when I was able to begin what was to be a fascinating and productive period of collaboration with Agnes Hung-Chong Chan, my colleague here in the Hong Kong Polytechnic University.

I had always felt that the way to improve the standard of Chinese-

English literary translation would be for native English speakers to collaborate with native Chinese speakers in small teams: as a non-native speaker, I will never be able to read the Chinese text with enough subtlety or depth; conversely, the Chinese speaker will find it extremely difficult to render the richness of the text in an English sufficiently nuanced to have literary value. Yet together, what might we not achieve? The reader will judge us on the product of this joint venture, of course, but I think the process of translating this book has been a very interesting and highly affirmative experience, and in terms of our collaboration, a resounding success.[5]

How did we work? Agnes Chan took on the painful job of slowly reading through the Chinese text, noting ambiguities, intertextualities, cruxes and challenges (of which more later). She then presented me with first drafts in English, including alternative readings and helpful notes on every page. Once a week, we would sit down together and slowly read through her draft, as I polished the English drafts, looking for rhythm, nuance, and cadence, as well as trying to create for our English versions a sound structure that could in some sense replicate or parallel the sounds of the original (a few of the more problematic poems will be discussed below). We were not always in agreement, though our collaboration was good-humoured: from time to time we did, however, come close to losing our patience with the poet, who tormented us with such seemingly intractable problems – but that is a fact of life, if you are foolish enough to attempt the charmingly impossible trade of poetry translation.

Yang Lian is engaged in testing the limits of his language, and in so doing, he has tested the limits of our ingenuity. Some of the problems we have had to deal with are acrostics (the three poems in the final section which all bear the title 詩 'poetry'), neologisms, coinages and apparent malapropisms (e.g. *oysterses*), the splitting of words into their component parts and even the splitting of characters into their constituents (Yang cites one example in his preface). These are tricky to negotiate, though not impossible to resolve.

However, there is one poem, one of the first I attempted, where we are presented with the conundrum of how to translate a text which has strict form but no content at all. 'SWAY' is a metrically perfect example of the form known as *Song ci*, which is to say, it is a lyric poem whose structure is based round a fixed pattern (once that of the original song which gave each pattern its title).[6] Now that pattern can't be reproduced in English, because it relates to patterns of tones, the fixed pitch contours (level, rising, dipping, falling) which every Chinese syllable has and no English syllable can have. Yang tells me that his intention in this poem was '...to show the pure sound-level in the Chinese language and poetry by distorting (taking off, breaking) the levels of Visual-links and Mean-ing-links of the characters, thus this is a poem of PURE SOUND'.[7]

What to do? My earliest draft simply translated word for word, with neither rhyme nor rhythm; second-stage drafts added some manipulation of word order and sense to give the same rhyme pattern as the original, and a similar rhythm:

WHO

smoke mouth in front night found
mountains he morning grand
labour text hand autumn round
ocean knife dream never sand
clothes ghost sweet tall sound

all slaughter year dark mound
bitter after blue-green band
not stone brow stand small ground
beauty come bitter black brand
word water bug million resound

Although I was not entirely successful in avoiding collocation (it is very hard to stop words from *meaning*: Yang tells me that writing the original took a great deal of effort, for the same reason), this was, I felt, enough to be going on with...but memories of Louis and Celia Zukofsky's *Catullus* kept running in my mind. So next I attempted to invoke the sound of the Chinese as the basis for the subsequent version, by substituting English words as close as I could find to the sound of the Chinese (this is difficult, because Chinese doesn't allow consonant clusters, and syllables can end only in vowels or nasals, and never in consonants):

SWAY

yank oh yeah you chin
fen sought a sham
lowing choose oh you eddying yam
more high easy door yo men
equal gog gun

106

sigh you antonian
squeak couching wan
domey bushy shocking land
choosy coolie herring lay
this way chawing chin

Not altogether bad, I thought, almost prepared to leave it there, even though the rhyme-scheme was under-developed. Yang Lian, however, suggested that I combine the two approaches, to produce a text which made no sense, yet had a structure which was clearly visible in English. After much experiment, and many dead-ends, I found the Welsh bardic metre *Cyhydedd Hir*,[8] which is composed of an octave stanza of two quatrains with a strict rhyme-scheme: near enough, we thought, with a little bending and stretching, to give us the final version. The title, by the way, had to change from the original 'WHO', which is the sense of the Chinese, to something closer to *shui*, the sound of the original.

SWAY

yank so yeah you chin
fen sought bam show shin
choose ewe add fling sin
moat high ease door fin
eik wall gun gog

sigh you anti dan
squeak couching ban
doe hay bushy shan
coolie herring fan
fizz way chaw cog

Equally puzzling was 'KNOWING', which in the original looks like this:

The characters are in the archaic Seal Script, and are just about intelligible to modern readers, with the exception of the central one, which is Yang Lian's own invention.[9] It is pronounced *yi*, and is composed of the archaic characters for *sun*, *person*, and *one*,[10] with the sense of 'the unity of Heaven and Man'.[11] The translator's goal here is to produce a text for the English reader at the same level of near-intelligibility (or near unintelligibility) as that intended for the Chinese reader, together with something of the same feeling of an archaic talisman or charm: the result is more graphic art than translation, some might say. The choice of Greek words rendered in the Latin alphabet was the solution I finally arrived at in 2000, after pondering other alternatives for a year or two. My thanks are due to my most erudite friend Lisa Raphals of UCR for her help with the Greek.

These two examples are probably quite enough detail for now, and there remain only a couple of final samples to be displayed to the weary reader. First is the sequence 'A LABYRINTH GRADUALLY GROWING', where each poem on the sequence has as its epigraph one line from 登高 'High Up', a well-known classical poem by the Tang dynasty master, Du Fu.[12] The two central couplets of poem read as follows in our translation:

> infinity of fallen leaves rustling, rustling
> ceaseless river waves rolling, rolling
> constantly travelling a million miles of autumn melancholy
> mounting this balcony alone in years of sickness

This exquisite little poem, written in the classical '7-character line' alluded to in 'CONSTRUCTED COMEDY', and of which Du Fu was such a master, is immediately accessible and instantly recognisable to the Chinese reader. The problem with this kind of intertextuality is that it doesn't translate: though he is a poet of world class who deserves to be much more widely known, how many English readers will actually know of Du Fu? Some may recall the 'Tu Fu' of Arthur Cooper and David Hawkes, or, more recently, David Hinton.[13] Disguised by two different spelling systems, it is the same poet. The crux of the problem for us is that, as translators, we cannot in English bring the combined notes of august authority and schoolroom familiarity which are inherent in the Chinese text: had we chosen to substitute for Du Fu, say a sonnet by Shakespeare (and we did consider that), then we would have had the familiarity and the authority, but at the price of losing the coherence between poem and epigraph, not to mention – dare I say it? – the authenticity of the work. But here I am in danger of straying into the deep waters inhabited by theorists, and

I will say no more. Yang explains it like this: 'what I did here was to "respond to" his poem in a creative way – my four poems are contemporary echoes of his lines, so finally the creative link has been built, and all the poems are joined together as one piece – the time-difference (THE TIME) has been cancelled!'[14]

Another interesting issue of intertextuality arises in the concluding section of 'RONDO AND COUNTERPOINT', where the poet begins to write an old-fashioned kind of Literary Chinese reminiscent of the great stylist Ban Gu (AD 32-92), author of the *History of the Former Han Dynasty*. This is very different to the Modern Standard Chinese employed elsewhere, and we wanted to make this obvious to the English reader, but were having problems deciding exactly how to do that. Help came from Francis R. Jones of the University of Newcastle upon Tyne, himself an extraordinarily gifted translator of poetry: the passage beginning '*Ban-Goo* read out these Wordes by Candle-light...' was transformed by Francis into a splendid Augustan English which beautifully parallels Ban Gu's lucid and elegant Chinese (and we thank him heartily for it). Now to the hoary old chestnuts of word-for-word and sense-for-sense transla-tion, we have added parody-for-parody.

It is our hope that we have succeeded in making a kind of sense of these very difficult and daring poems, and that some of what makes them difficult and daring in Chinese will be at least dimly visible in our English text. I will say nothing of the many allusions – to places, writers, artists, landscapes – made tiresomely obscure by the awkwardness of the transliteration of foreign names in Chinese; nor will I dwell on the many allusions to the ancient and book-haunted culture of China: fewer of them than we hoped have survived the transition to English, though one possible excep-tion may be the title of 'GAIA'. The original Chinese term *kun* 坤 is a complex one: it is the name for the second hexagram of the ancient Book of Change (*Yi Jing* aka *I Ching*), and represents the cosmic principle of Earth, the physical manifestation of the energy of Yin. Gaia in both her ancient and her modern senses of goddess of the earth and hypothetical principle of ecological balance, though perhaps more personalised than the Chinese *kun*, at least captures something of the numinosity of the term.

Perhaps Yang Lian's poetry can show us that, if we stretch language to its breaking point, we will be able to glimpse behind the straining structure of the known a new kind of poetry, an anti-poetry defined by the absences and silences of the poetry we knew. This has been the object of the journey we have undertaken, stress-testing both our languages as we went, in the effort to delineate a diagram of the very strange world that is the poetry of Yang Lian, across whose exotic waters we have voyaged, alternately dazed and delighted.

BRIAN HOLTON
Hong Kong

1. *Yi*, bilingual edition, tr. Mabel Lee (Green Integer, Los Angeles, 2002).

2. As he points out in his Preface, above.

3. Yang Lian: *Where the Sea Stands Still: New Poems*, tr. Brian Holton (Bloodaxe Books, 1999), p.139.

4. *The Poetics of Exile*: School of European Languages and Literatures, University of Auckland, New Zealand, July 2003, wonderfully organised by Mike Hanne and his team.

5. Though please, before you judge, reader, recall John Dryden: 'But slaves we [translators] are, and labour on another man's plantation; we dress the vineyard, but the wine is the owner's: if the soil be sometimes barren, then we are sure of being scourged; if it be fruitful, and our care succeeds, we are not thanked; for the proud reader will say, the poor drudge has done his duty...' (Preface to *Ovid's Epistles*, 1680).

6. This particular example is, as they say 'written to' Langtao Sha or Waves on the Sand: note that the content normally bears no resemblance to the title. It's as if we were to write a new set of words to the tune of a well-known song.

7. Personal communication: e-mail 4 December 2004. Yang explains this and much more (in Chinese) at http://www.poemlife.com.cn/forum/add.jsp?forumID=31&page=1&msgID=2147483420

8. Thanks to Lewis Turco: his *Book of Forms* (University Press of New England, 2000) is a gem of a book. You will find *Cyhydedd Hir* on pp. 162-63.

9. The system for making new Chinese characters is no longer productive (with the possible exception of names for chemical elements), so it is a radical and shocking step to attempt to add a new character to the corpus. How can we render that innovative boldness in the text?

10. 日, 人 and — in their modern forms.

11. *Yi*, bilingual edition, tr. Mabel Lee (Green Integer, Los Angeles, 2002), p.343. In a personal communication, Yang also says 'the reason I put the character I invented for YI at the center of the ring-characters, is to point out the link between the two most important works of mine (*Yi* and *Concentric Circles*), in order to build up the inner-structured Poetry-

world of mine: it is another level of 'Concentric Circles' – Inside and Outside of China, Inside and Outside of one's own languages – the real journey toward to the open-ended question of Poetry ——— POETRY IS' (e-mail, 4 December 2004).

12. See David Hawkes: *A Little Primer of Tu Fu* (OUP 1967; Renditions Press, 1990), pp.203-04, 'From A Height'; and Arthur Cooper: *Li Po and Tu Fu* (Penguin Classics, 1973), pp.227-28, also 'From A Height'.

13. *The Selected Poems of Tu Fu* (Anvil Press, 1990).

14. Personal communication: e-mail 4 December 2004. Yang has also written an interesting discussion and exegesis of this poem (in English), in the *Capstone Journal* (2003): see http://inside.bard.edu/capstonejournal/2003/df-index.htm

www.ingramcontent.com/pod-product-compliance
Lightning Source LLC
Jackson TN
JSHW011351130125
77033JS00015B/561